And *You* Think *He* Doesn't Exist

MICHELLE LOVE

ISBN 978-1-0980-9269-6 (paperback)
ISBN 978-1-0980-9270-2 (digital)

Christian Faith Publishing, Inc.
832 Park Avenue
Meadville, PA 16335
www.christianfaithpublishing.com

Printed in the United States of America

I find joy in every day,
not because life is always good,
but because God is.

Preface

An amazing, unbelievable, and unexplainable way that God shows you that you are exactly where you are meant to be.

And You Think He Doesn't Exist is a true and enlightening story of a family who took a road trip and had to endure a few stumbling blocks while trying to reach their destination. In the story, the family is faced with an unexpected change. Eventually, one of the characters tries to deal with what transpired and writes what she has learned from her experience of it all.

When you read this book, you will discover for yourself how to deal with things that God may have shown you that you could not quite understand, or maybe you did not believe in what you saw.

Acknowledgments

⚜

This book is dedicated to Tommy Stone and my grandchildren, Javion, Jamari, and Jaiouni Hendrix, who endured this horrific but blessed journey along with me. Mimi loves you! Also, to my two daughters, Mykisha Walton and Shikoya Hartley, who I am profoundly grateful for. I could only imagine how you two felt seeing us all in the state that we were in, especially you, Kisha, who stood to lose not only your mother but all three of your children at the same time. To Taraji Walton Simmons and Micki Hartley, who was riding in the other car unharmed, praise God, it could have been you!

To my husband, Willie Love; my sister, Deborah Davis; my son, Kenneth Walton Jr.; and the rest of my immediate family and friends, whose enthusiasm for this story encouraged me to write this book, I thank you all, and to God be the glory!

Chapter 1

Yay, it is Friday, and the weekend will begin! I only have four more hours until my shift is over, and my three-day vacation starts. I am so excited for our family road trip to our annual family reunion, which will be held in Albuquerque this year. As I am sitting in the breakroom eating my lunch, I think about our trip. I find myself contemplating on whether I should rent a minivan so that Tommy, my children, my grandchildren, and myself will all travel in one vehicle, or should we drive our own vehicles? If we drive Tommy's truck and Koya drives her car like they suggest, we can save money since our finances are a little tight. Welp… I finish eating lunch, and now it is time for me to get back to my gate and work my flight.

Next to my gate is my friend Jenny, working her flight. As we are preparing our paperwork for our flights, I mention to Jenny about me going on this short three-day vacation with my children and grandchildren and how excited I am to be going. I am telling her how undecided I am about perhaps renting a minivan versus just driving Tommy's truck and my daughter Koya's car, which will save us money, and we can do more on our trip. Jenny asks me how reliable the truck is. I tell her that Tommy has mentioned that the truck is reliable. So she says to me, "Just rent a car," and we both continue to complete our flights.

My shift is finally over, and I am walking out saying my good-byes to all my coworkers as I usually do, and I hear Jenny yell out to me, "Rent the car!" in a loud voice. I chuckle, wave my hand at her, and proceed to walk up the hallway to the sky train, which takes me to where I park my car.

When I arrive home, I am greeted by Tommy, and he asks me how my day was at work. I tell him that I had a good day, but I am ready to go on our trip. I ask him if he has checked everything out as far as the fluids and all on the truck so that we will be ready to leave in the morning. He replies yes, but he will probably need to go get another tire for the back driver's side of the truck in the morning prior to us leaving. We say our goodnights to each other and go to bed.

It's approximately 6:00 a.m. when I wake up. I lean over toward Tommy and tell him to wake up, that it's time to get up so he can go get the tire for the truck, and we can get started on our trip. I also call both my daughters, Kisha and Koya, and tell them to wake up, get the kids together, and meet at my house. That way, we can all leave at the same time. When Tommy comes back from getting the tire, he and I begin loading the truck with our luggage, snacks, pillows, and anything else we think will make our trip comfortable. I am going over my checklist in my head, making sure that we do not forget anything. The girls arrive in Koya's car that she will be driving since I have decided not to rent the minivan. Both car and truck have been checked out, and we are now ready to begin our road trip. I yell out to everybody, "Let's hit the road!" No one else is as excited as I am while they are all still in sleep mode.

Tommy and I are in the truck, along with my two granddaughters. Kisha and her two boys and Koya and her infant are all in the same car. As we pull out of the driveway, with Koya following close behind, I begin praying, asking God to give us traveling grace to make it to our destination safely. The tanks in both cars are filled with gas, and we are headed toward the Interstate 17 North toward Flagstaff, Arizona. I am trying to keep everybody awake and excited like me, so I suggest we sing songs, you know, like road trip songs! I start singing "Row Row Row Your Boat" and ask them to follow me singing so that we will be singing what you call a round. Laughing at our silly singing of what we call road trip songs, we then start enjoying the scenery, admiring the beautiful mountains in Arizona. The kids are excited to see some wildlife such as deer, cows, and buffalos that they have spotted. After a few hours of traveling, the singing is over, and the girls are sound asleep. Tommy is still driving, checking in his rearview mirror, making sure Koya is still close behind. We continue driving, trying to make some headway.

Somewhere outside of Grants, New Mexico, we stop to fill the cars up with gas, stretch our legs, and grab a bite to eat. We get back into the cars, heading toward the highway, and the truck begins to cut out and cut off. *Oh no!* I am thinking to myself. Meanwhile, Tommy is trying several times to start the car, and it will not start. Now I am saying out loud, "You have got to be kidding me!" We have already missed Friday meet and greet for our family reunion because I had to work, and now, we are going to miss the family picnic at the park and possibly the banquet dinner if we do not get this car started! Keep in mind, this is 2016, and it's hard to find good help these days; people are not as trusting as they used to be, so everybody is passing us by. Koya's car is entirely too small to transport everybody, so Tommy and Koya drive to find help while the rest of us wait in the truck.

Tommy spots a nearby auto garage and has the truck towed there, only to find out that there is no mechanic on duty who can fix the fuel pump that they say goes out of the truck. They will try to call someone in to fix the truck; however, it is going to take a few hours to fix it. Now I am livid! "A few hours?" I yell! We will never make it to enjoy the family reunion! You know what thoughts are going through my mind right now? All I can hear is Jenny's voice telling me to rent a car! So I thought, *Okay, no worries. I will just go rent a car because there is no way all of us are going to fit into Koya's car, and we need to get going so that we can get to Albuquerque.* So I begin asking around for the nearest rental car company. Only to be told that there is not any. I repeat, there are no rental car companies at all in that city. I am thinking, *Now what?* to myself, trying not to get even more upset. I call my sister, who is already there in Albuquerque, enjoying herself with all the family stuff! I tell her that the truck breaks down, and it is going to take a few hours to get fixed.

She asks, "Where are you?"

"Somewhere outside of Grants," I reply. She makes mention to some of our family members that our truck has broken down, and one of my cousins volunteers to come get us. I decline his offer because I thought why should he have to miss out on all the festivities due to our truck breaking down. *I should have rented a rental car!* I am shouting in my head! I can just kick myself in the butt! So as angry as I am with myself, I have decided that we will just make the best out of our troubles and wait until someone could come and fix the truck and get us back on the road again. After all, what more do we have to lose? We are already missing the family picnic at the park. Hopefully, by the time the truck gets fixed, we will at least be able to make it in time to enjoy the banquet dinner.

So we wait, we wait, and we wait. Finally, someone arrives, who thinks—yeah, that is right; I said he *thinks*—he can fix the fuel pump. Hmm…still trying not to upset myself anymore or anyone else for that matter, we try to make the best out of the situation. Tommy is helping the mechanic put the fuel pump into the truck, and Koya decides that she will start weaving Kisha's hair. Yep, that is what I said. *Weave* Kisha's hair! She is going to add some hair extensions to Kisha's hair while we are sitting outside of the car in a deserted restaurant parking lot, with a few transients or bums! Mad as all get out, I sigh and take a deep breath and go to where my grandkids are so that I can try and keep them entertained. We find a dollar store and go inside to find us something to buy to keep us from being so bored. The kids have started running around and playing with each other. I decide to go check on Tommy and see how the truck is coming along. They are getting it together, and it should not be that much longer.

I go back to where my daughters are, still at a loss for words, looking at them holding up these strands and wefts full of hair. I am laughing to myself, thinking there is a horse out there somewhere missing a tail! Then I have to think and say I cannot talk I have a fake ponytail in my head myself! After laughing, I start to feel a little better, and I am not so angry anymore. Whew! I finally calm down! I sit down on the curb with my daughters, watching my grandkids play, and just wanting all of this to hurry up and be over with so that we can be on our way.

While sitting there, I am greeted by a couple of homeless Native American Indians, who stop and ask if we have any food and drinks.

I reply yes and give them some of our food, drinks, and snacks. I ask them if they know God. They reply, "Yes, we know God." I then begin conversing with them, and from time to time, I glance over at Kisha, and she will give me a look that could kill! I smile and turn back to continue talking. I begin singing gospel songs, and the Native Americans join me in singing. What a beautiful sound as we sit singing, passing the time away.

Again, I glance at Kisha. This time, she asks me in a rather frustrating, irritating tone, "Oh my god, Mom, you are so embarrassing! Why would you sit and sing with complete strangers?" and shakes her head. I chuckle and keep singing. Koya is still weaving Kisha's hair; our Native American friends have now sat down and joined us. The kids are sitting in the car, and Tommy is still in the auto shop, helping them work on the fuel pump.

Finally, two and a half to three hours later, the truck is finally finished! "Yay," I scream, "let us get this show back on the road!" We say goodbye to our newfound friends; Koya has finished Kisha's hair; we load up the kids; and we are on our way again.

Approximately two hours later, we arrive at Isleta Casino and Hotel in Albuquerque, where our family banquet dinner is underway! We hurry up, run upstairs to our hotel room to get cleaned up, and change into our formal clothing. We made it just in time for the dinner. We are greeted by our family, who are all so happy to know that we made it there safe and sound. There are some family members we have not seen in years, and there are even family members that we have never met before. Family mingling and sitting around; watching the children running around and playing with their cousins; everybody laughing, dancing, drinking, doing what families do—I am saying to myself, what a blessing it is that we made it and just being able to be here, enjoying the rest of the evening with family.

Chapter 2

Waking up Sunday morning and seeing what is in the plans for today, we notice that some of the family members are going to the park, while others are going to attend church. I chose to go attend services at Bethlehem Baptist Church where I grew up in. I am excited to go! I have not been to that church since I was sixteen years old, which is thirty-seven years ago! I want my children and my grandchildren to see the church that my sisters, my brother, and I were raised in as children. What an awesome experience! The building brings back so many memories as my sister and I sit there, reminiscing about things that happened with us in that church back in the day when we were kids. While in the meantime, the preacher is preaching, and I am not hearing nor paying attention at all to what that pastor is preaching. Shame on me!

Once the church service is over, we head over to my aunt's house, which is right up the street, to change clothes so that we can go to the park and join the rest of the family for the barbeque. We arrive at the park; the weather is beautiful! The sun is shining but not too hot, and my goodness, the smell of barbecue is all in the air! My cousin Charles has parked his truck with this huge mobile grill attached to the back of the truck, smelling all good and stuff! There is music playing, a few card games going on, dominos, and drones flying around taking pictures or videos of what is going on. Children are getting acquainted with one another, running around playing, and grown-ups are doing grown-up things, if you know what I mean. It is so nice getting caught up on what is going on in everybody's lives these days; we are having some good old family fun!

Our bellies are now full of all the delicious food that is cooked by our cousin Charles—ribs, hot links, chicken, potato salad, etc.; you know how black folks do it. And now, we have caught what some folks call the—itis, which means we are full, sleepy, and ready to retire! We begin saying our goodbyes and hugging everyone, telling each other, "Until next time," which will be in the year 2018 in our hometown, Phoenix. We gather up my grandkids and load up the truck and car, and head over to my aunt Esther's house, where we will be staying for the night.

Chapter 3

❦

"Rise and shine!" I say to Tommy, waking him up. "Let us all go grab some breakfast and head back home to Phoenix." While getting breakfast, I receive a phone call from my cousin Sharon, who says that a lot of the family are hanging out at my uncle Bo's house, and we should stop by before getting on the road, so we did. When we arrive at my uncle's house, a lot of my family members are just hanging out in the front yard, listening to music, and my aunt Brenda is fixing brats sausages and some other food to eat while we are hanging out. My uncle Bo is in the house (he has been sick earlier that year), so I go inside to check on him to see how he has been doing. After chitchatting with my uncle and other family members, I go to Tommy to tell him that we should be making our way to the highway. As I am getting ready to get in the car, we hear the song "Walking the Dog" by Rufus Thomas! "Oh Lord," I yell, "that was the song!" My cousin Sharon and I start doing the dance to that song, and I am showing my kids how our parents used to dance off that song back in the day. We laugh, and my kids laugh at us at how we are dancing! Now time is starting to get away from us, and we really need to get on the road. I say, "Goodbye, everybody," and we leave.

We stop by the gas station to fill up both vehicles and start making our way back to Phoenix. Once again, it's Tommy, my two grand-daughters, and myself in the truck and my three grandsons and Kisha are in the car with Koya, who is following closely behind. I say my prayers again, asking God to give us traveling grace to make it back home safe, and off we go. We are on I-40 on our way toward Flagstaff when suddenly Tommy says, "Your brother tells me it's quicker to go through Payson." So he calls my brother and asks him about going through Payson.

My brother replies, "Yes, it is quicker," and tells us which route to take. So now we're on our way to Highway 87 through Payson. I have never been on this route before. It is beautiful! Tommy and I are admiring the beauty of all the trees, mountains, and the series of roads going up and over the Magollon Rim into the vast pine forest of eastern Arizona. *Wow, this is gorgeous!* Just looking off the side of the road as to how deep some of the valleys are, I say to Tommy, "God is so amazing. Look at all this that he has created. How can a person not believe in God?"

He agrees with me saying, "Yes, it is amazing!"

So now we start thinking of things that God has done that makes him so amazing in many ways. So just to name a few, I say, "Yeah, like how he makes a woman's breast fill up with milk when the baby cries when they're hungry."

Tommy says, "Yeah, like how he makes a penis fit inside a vagina, how the sperm fertilizes an egg and creates a baby (typical man's theory)!"

So I say, "Yeah, how he knows the very number of hairs that is in your head. How he makes your brain, your lungs, your heart, shoot, how he just created! Yeah, I say he is amazing!"

We notice we are getting low on gas, so we decide to stop at this convenience store to gas up, stretch our legs, and this time, we will switch kids since we are approximately forty-five minutes away from Phoenix. Koya will take her daughter, and we will take Kisha and her three children with us, which will make it easier so that Koya does not have to pass her side of town to take Kisha home. I make sure the kids are in the truck and make sure that their seatbelts are fastened, and we are good to go. At this point, Kisha has decided she will just ride with Koya because she wants to smoke, and she knows there is no smoking in the truck with me! Since we are so close to reaching Phoenix, Koya proceeds to drive ahead of us instead of following us this time around.

As we are driving along, I am still admiring the beauty of the mountains and all, and then I begin singing gospel songs. Tommy joins me, and the grandkids are just sitting in the back, listening. Suddenly, I hear a very loud pop! Tommy looks at me, and I look at him; it appears to me that the truck is going sideways, the tire in the back on the driver's side has blown out, and the rubber from the tire gets caught underneath the axle, causing the truck to flip over. Everything happens so fast, and now suddenly, I am flipping over and over; it seems as though the flipping will not stop! *Dear God, what is happening!* Finally, the flipping stops. There is dirt and glass everywhere, and I can hear the kids in the back yelling. Du (my oldest grandson) is not in the car! They are crying frantically and screaming—they have seen their brother fly out of the window! Du has been ejected out of the back window of the truck.

I notice that, for some reason, I cannot move; I cannot turn to see my grandkids. *Please, God, tell me what is going on!* I keep repeating to myself. *Please, help me!* I am yelling to myself! I can see Tommy to my left trying to climb out of the window of the driver's side; you can tell that he is in a lot of pain trying to do so—pain is written all over his face. He says, "I need to go find Du." I can hear Tommy yelling and screaming for my grandson. Then I can hear Tommy saying, "Oh God, oh God, please help me!"

At that moment, I began praying to God, "Dear God, please do not let me lose my grandson, please!"

Du says, "Here I am. I'm over here!"

Tommy shouts out, "Here he is. I found Du, and he's alright!"

I am saying to myself, *Praise God!* My grandson has landed on a rock several feet away from where the truck has landed. His right arm is broken so bad that when you try picking him up, his arm and shoulder just roll around backward. Can you imagine seeing that? Tommy then comes to the passenger side of truck where I am and tells me to close my eyes. He says that I have a lot of dirt all over me, and that he is going to pour water over me to rinse my face off. I close my eyes, and I can feel the water running down my face. I am not sure where Tommy goes after that because I have not heard anymore from him. I am told that I have been going in and out of consciousness.

As I am sitting there again, I am still in and out of consciousness. I hear a man's voice at my window, and he says to me, "What can I do to help?"

At this time, I cannot actually see this man, but I can hear him. It is so hard for me to talk, but I manage to get out, "Please, save my grandkids."

The next thing that I see is this man—he is a rather large man, or should I say, he is very tall with big broad shoulders, and he has a lot of white, white curly hair. His hair is so white, almost as if it has light in it. I am saying to myself, *Dang, this man's hair is white!* Anyway, that man never says a word, but he is holding my granddaughter. I must say she is holding on to him for dear life! She has wrapped herself around him so tight, and it appears that she is okay, just very scared and shaken up! Once again, I cannot speak for whatever reason, but to me, I acknowledge to him that I thank him for saving my granddaughter.

Meanwhile, I can hear my other grandson crying and yelling behind me. He says, "Mimi, why won't you save me!" He says, "Please, please, save me. Why won't you save me, Mimi!"

That is very painful for me to hear. But for some reason again, I am not able to speak or move to let my grandson know that I will save him, but I can't. I am thinking to myself, *Why is it that I cannot move or speak? What has happened to me?* Can you imagine how painful it is to hear your grandchild in pain, and you are right there in his sight, but you cannot say or do anything to help him! God knows I will lay down my life for my grandchildren! I feel so helpless and angry at the same time. I cannot understand what is going on. Now I am gritting my teeth, fighting hard, and trying with all my might to move, or just to be able to say something to my grandson, and I cannot! In my mind, I am saying, *Lord, please help me. Please!* but I cannot move.

I look to my left, and I can see a lady, and she says, "I will save you. I am a nurse, and I'm going to climb back there with you and stay with you until someone comes to help you."

My grandson, whose nickname is Hov, is in the middle of the truck, and that part of the truck has caved in from the impact of the truck flipping and pins him where he cannot move and cannot get out. His lips are slashed, and he has multiple other cuts and bruises. Then there is a woman who comes to my window, and she asks me how I am doing. Now for whatever reason, I can speak. I say to her that I am in a lot of pain, and that I have not experienced so much pain before in my life! She asks me what my name is. I reply, "It is Michelle."

And she says, "My name is Michelle also."

Then she asks me if I am a believer. I answer, "Yes, I am."

So she says, "Good. I am going to stay right here praying for you until help comes along. Now I understand that there are people there who has formed a prayer chain and began praying for me and my family. I never see them.

If you remember, I have mentioned earlier in the story that my daughters, Koya and Kisha, are driving ahead of us, so Koya is looking in her rearview mirror to see if we are behind her, and she never sees the truck. So she makes several calls to my cell phone, and she gets no answer. She calls Tommy's phone, and again, no answer. So now, Koya realizes something is wrong. She pulls over on the side of the road, gets out, and flags down a car that is coming down the street approximately three minutes behind her. The car stops and a gentleman gets out of his car, and she asks him if he has seen a silver truck back there anywhere. The gentleman does not say a word. He just puts his head down, and Koya says, "What is it? What's wrong?"

He replies and says to her, "There has been a terrible accident with the silver truck."

Right away, Koya goes back to her car and tries to calm down Kisha, who is losing it because she hears what the gentleman has said. They both realize something is not good with us. Suddenly, Koya sees a police car race past her, so she begins to follow the police car in the opposite direction. They follow the police to where our accident has taken place. You can see that the truck has gone over the side of the guard rail and has landed down a mountain or ravine. Koya and Kisha begin to run down the mountain frantically, yelling and screaming, "Mom!" No answer. Kisha sees her son Javion, whose nickname is Du, laying on a rock. She also sees her other son Jamari, whose nickname is Hov, pinned in the truck along with me. She notices Tommy is laying on the ground as well, and he is in excruciating pain. She goes to get Jaiouni, her daughter, from the man who has rescued her from the truck. Jaiouni is still frightened and very shook up. She goes with Kisha hesitantly. When Kisha takes her daughter in her arms, my granddaughter says to Kisha, "Grandma had me."

Kisha, looking at her somewhat confused and dumbfounded, asks her what she is talking about. Kisha replies and asks if she is talking about Mimi. My granddaughter says, "No, not Mimi. Grandma Simms!"

Kisha, being perplexed or disconcerted at what she hears her daughter say, thought to herself, *She could not possibly have been with her grandma Simms because she passed away approximately three months or so ago.* Kisha is thinking and asking herself, *Why would my four-year-old baby say something like that? She is just four years old, and that is not something that a four-year-old would just make up to say. Could this be possible that her grandma did have her? Everyone else in the truck had severe to fatal injuries. How did Jaiouni escape without any injuries?*

Koya is trying her best to keep calm and help in any way that she can. She tries to talk to me, and she gets no response. She says that I finally looks up at her and tells her, "Tell my sister Deborah that I beat her."

That is a term used by my sister and I—what we will say to each other—if one of us should die first. We will say, "Ha! I beat you." So I tell Koya to tell my sister that I beat her, and then I went unconscious again. Koya yells and yells at me, and still no response. She says she begins to pray for me, and then she remembers that I hate the *f*-word. So she says she yells out "F——!" She yells that *f*-word three times, and instantly, I open my eyes and give her a look she said that could kill! *How are you praying and swearing at the same time?* She apologizes for saying that word, but she says she needs to get my attention and try to keep me from slipping back into unconsciousness.

It appears that a lot of time has passed, and still no helicopters or paramedics has come. Everyone is concerned about me because I am not responding, and I keep slipping in and out of consciousness.

While being in an unconscious state, I cannot hear anything, but I remember seeing my step-grandson (Dajon) in a tunnel, and he is waving at me to come to him. I am looking at him, and I am trying so hard to get to him. I am reaching my arm out to him, and he is reaching his arm out to me so that we can grab each other's hand. But the tunnel is moving, and he is going further and further away from me. I say to him, "I'm coming, baby!" Unfortunately, I can never reach him. Now, in my conscious state of mind, I know that he passed away approximately a year or so prior to our accident. My stepdaughter was devasted by the loss of her son, and it hurt me deeply to know what she was going through as I could not imagine losing my child. I knew him and spent some time with him, but we were not that close to one another, so it is rather strange that I will see him, and he is beckoning for me.

Finally, the helicopters and ambulance arrive. I am still not able to move, and I can rarely talk. I hear something that sounds like a saw and a lot of loud noise as if the truck is being torn apart. I am being extricated—both my grandson and I have to be extricated. Tommy, both of my grandsons, and I are transported to the hospital by helicopter, and my granddaughter is transported in the ambulance, along with my daughter Kisha. Koya, with her two children in her car, are following the ambulance to the hospital. As they place me on the stretcher and put me into the helicopter, I remember telling God, "You know I hate helicopters!"

That is all I remember about the helicopter ride, and then I hear the paramedics say, "You're here!" which means, I have arrived at Maricopa County Hospital in Phoenix.

Chapter 4

⸺ ❧ ⸺

I am guessing that I am now in the emergency room somewhere; I can hear a lot of talking around me, and I can even hear Tommy screaming, but I am still unable to see any of this going on. I am not sure how much time has passed, or what is going on for that matter. I have no idea where my grandchildren are, or where my children are. I am thinking, *Where is my mom, and does she know where I am and what is happening to me?* I can hear people praying over me, and I also hear and can recognize one of my coworkers Deryck saying, "Give me a towel so that I can get this dirt off her because she is never dirty like this!"

I am thinking to myself, *Thank you, bro. Get the dirt off me please!* Again, I never see him. I also remember hearing the voice of my pastor from my church, Pastor James Preston, also praying in my right ear, although I never see him, but I could hear his voice, and for whatever reason, the image of my pastor in my head at that time stood big! I mean, huge! So big, it is unbelievable, and he stands over the back side of my bed where I am lying. It's as though he is protecting me. At least, that is how I feel. It is hard to explain, but I just know and feel that he is there to form a hedge of protection over me.

I remember the doctor speaking to me as well—I can only hear him, but I cannot see him either. He says to me, "Your back and neck are so severed that I do not think I am able to fix it, and most likely, your outcome will be death."

I am thinking, *Okay*...so I ask him, "How much time do I have?"

He says, "I need to perform a surgery as soon as possible, so about two hours."

I reply, "Okay then, I will need to call my mother and my father."

And right away, I hear a voice of a female on my left, saying, "I am right here with a phone. Give me the phone numbers, and I will make the calls for you. The doctor then asks me to sign the paperwork for him to perform the surgery. I sign it. At that moment, I begin to pray over that doctor's hand who was going to perform surgery on me. I believe I went to sleep because the next thing I remember is my father crying and holding my hand, and he does not want to let go of my hand. I tell him not to worry about me because either way it goes, or however it turns out, I am going to be okay.

The surgery is performed, and I wake up in the ICU. The doctor informs my family that the surgery went well, and that I should be in the ICU for a month, and then I will have to go to rehabilitation for three months for therapy. I stay in the ICU for approximately seven days before I am moved into my own room. Once in my own room, I wake up and discover this big apparatus on my head. It is called a halo. Oh my! I am thinking, *I have to walk around with this big thing on my head! How am I supposed to balance myself with this big thing!* My mother, my sister, my brother, my dad, my stepmother, my daughters, and Tommy are all there in my room with me when the doctors come in to explain to me about what has happened, and why I am now wearing a halo. I have broken my neck, my back, and several ribs in the accident. I have three titanium rods that are holding me together, and some other nuts, bolts, and screws (which I refer to as my hardware) that will stay inside of me for the rest of my life, and I will have to wear this halo for three months.

I notice I have a lot of glass inside of my skin, on my neck, and arms that the nurse will try to remove little by little when they come in from time to time. She says that the glass needs to work its way out. I also notice that I am unable to move my left arm and hand. I am having trouble walking, so I have to use a walker. I am unable to bathe myself, and then I will keep one eye open at a time because it is just easier for me to see that way. I realize all these things that I am used to doing, I can no longer do anymore. I am always able to do for myself; I am Miss Independent! I like doing things on my own, and now this is all being taken away from me? I am thinking, *Now look at how life is going to be for me from here on out.* For instance, the idea of having someone to bathe me, or not being able to have full use of my left hand or arm. Also, having to walk with a walker. I am mortified! I mean, not that I think I am better than that, or I am feeling sorry for myself. It is something about being used to doing things on my own, and now, I have lost that ability to do so. I am thinking, *How am I to manage without doing these things?* It goes to show you that you should never take things for granted.

Then I ask about what has happened, and that's when Tommy explains to me about the accident. He says we had a blowout, and we flipped over and went down a ravine. I asks about my grandchildren, and I am told that all three of them are doing well, and they are home. Du (Javion) has broken his clavicle and his right arm, so he is wearing a cast for a few months. He also has a gash in the back of his head that requires stitches. He also has to get stitches on his ears, and there are some other scratches and bruises. He is hospitalized for two days. Hov (Jamari) has suffered a concussion, his lips are slashed from the impact, which requires stitches as well, plus he has several cuts, bruises, and scratches. He is hospitalized for one day. There are no serious injuries found on Jaiouni, my granddaughter, who we call Pooh. She has a few minor scratches on her hand, and that is all. Tommy is wearing what we call a turtle shell because he also has broken his back, but his injuries do not require surgery. He has to wear the turtle shell for six months. So after hearing all that, I sit back and try to process everything I have just heard, and now I am feeling rather empty inside.

Chapter 5

It is approximately day six, and I am still in the hospital. I have lots and lots of visitors from my family and friends—some I remember visiting, and some of them I do not. I am taking a lot of medication, which is keeping me drowsy and sleepy majority of the time. There are so many flowers in my room that it looks like a florist store, and it smells like one too! In fact, the florist from the hospital comes to my room and says that she must meet me because she has never seen so many people come and purchase so many flowers from the gift shop for just one room. She says to me, "I know your name is Michelle, and you also go by Regina. I know you work for Southwest Airlines, and that you are a very loved person."

She is right, I am very loved, and I have an awfully close and supportive family and an amazing group of friends that God has blessed me with. I am just feeling blessed all around! Even during feeling so blessed, my mind goes back to thinking about the accident. It just goes to prove that one minute you can be fine, and next minute, you are not. Or that tomorrow is not promised to you. Again, take nothing for granted and be grateful for all things. Not a day goes by without me thinking of what has transpired. In fact, I am told that the people driving in their cars behind us at the accident are a doctor, a nurse, two EMTs, and a fireman—all came to our aid and helped to rescue us until help arrived. I am told that the doctor had neck braces in his car, which he has placed on my grandsons' and myself. Just think about it, how many people carry neck braces in their car? Also, between the doctor, the nurse, the fireman, and EMTs, they have already started an IV on me and have all our information and vitals ready for the helicopter and ambulance when they arrive.

How blessed are we? I am thinking. God is so good; he sent all these angels to us! He didn't have to do it, but he did! He saves all of us! Despite my injuries and some small changes I must make in my life, I am grateful, profoundly grateful!

Day nine of being in the hospital, and I have been staying awake a little more than I have been. I am not eating that much; I do not have much of an appetite. All I really feel like eating are apples! I have started working on holding my left arm up and working on moving my hand before my dad comes to visit. Every time he comes to visit, the first thing that he has me doing is exercising my arm and hand (mind you, he visits me every day!). He raises up my arm and starts yelling at me not to let my arm drop! I am literally in tears trying to keep my arm up. Then he makes me open and close my hand over and over, until he feels I have done enough. He yells at me, "You will not lose use of your hand and your arm!" I do not want to lose use of my hand and arm either, so I try to do the best that I can in exercising them. The physical therapist comes in and will make me walk with the walker up and down the hallway two or three times a day. My mother comes to bathe me. She and Tommy make sure I am staying clean. My daughters try and comb the top part of what hair I have left after the doctor has shaved the back half of my head for the surgery. It is a little difficult for them to do because of the halo, but they do their best.

I am also able to stay awake enough during visits with friends and family for a little while longer these days. I have a surprise visitor today! It is Towanda, my best friend of twenty years. We started working at Southwest Airlines together, and then she moved away to North Carolina, so it has been years since I have seen her. What a surprise and blessing! She comes to visit me all the way from North Carolina, and she buys me an entire box of apples! You know, the kind of apples that come already sliced with caramel in a little plastic container? That is what she brings with her when she comes to visit me. I am so happy and grateful! That is all I wanted to eat, and I am extra excited to see my longtime friend as well.

It is late in the evening, and everyone has gone home. I am sitting in my bed, and I realize I must go to the bathroom. So I am looking at that walker, and I say to myself, "I can make it to the bathroom without that walker." And besides, no one is here with me to tell me not to, so I am going to try it. I take my time, and I slide my legs to the edge of the bed, and I sit there. Then I stand up to get my balance because I am not used to walking with this big ol' halo on my head, and I begin to slowly walk toward the bathroom. I made it, I used it, washed my hands, and I walked back to my bed! "You go, girl!" I tell myself. I am so excited; I knew I could do it! When my mother comes the next morning, I show her that I can walk without the walker, and I can use the bathroom by myself. Of course, she wants me to be careful. So I tell her that I want to try and wash myself. She stands by the door just in case I need her, and I am able to wash myself too! So amazed at the progress I am making, when the doctor has come in to do his normal routine as well as the physical therapist, I show them and tell them all that I can do by myself. So pleased, the therapist says she does not think she has to send me to a rehabilitation facility due to me having enough of family support. She says that with some restrictions, I should be able to go home tomorrow after the hanger guys come to tighten my halo.

Chapter 6

How excited I am to know that I am going home today. My mother arrives to give me a ride home, while Tommy and my father and stepmother go to my house to move furniture around and make sure that my hospital bed arrives, turning my living room into my now new bedroom. I am not able to be moved into my original bedroom because I am considered a fall risk, and my bedroom is upstairs, and I am unable to climb the stairs.

I arrive home, and everyone is there to make sure that I am comfortable, and everything I need is in proximity—my walker, this gripping metal stick that I am supposed to use if I need to grab or pick up things with (I call it my extra hands), a table full of medication, etc. I guess I am all set. My daughter Kisha and my grandkids are all there with me, as well as Tommy.

My family take shifts to take care of me every day, making sure I am taking my medication, eating, and washing up and all. How I long to take a hot shower, but because of the halo, I will not able to do so for three months. I sit on my hospital bed day in and day out, appreciating everything that everyone is doing for me, but I want to do things on my own. I need to do whatever I can to get myself back together. Not a day goes by without me thinking about the accident, and I just cry and pray, thanking God for all that he has done for me and my family.

All the medications that I am taking is keeping me drowsy and sleepy most of the day. I still have a lot of visitors coming by, offering their help, and bringing food for me and my family to eat. I still don't have much of an appetite. One of my coworkers, Vee, comes every

Wednesday with either baked goods or a meal. She is someone that I just speak to at work but never had a relationship with, and yet she comes every week. Yvonne, another coworker, also makes it her business to show up every week with food. How blessed do I feel to know that people love me enough to take time from their schedule and visit me on a weekly basis! I know my family has my back, but goodness, I cannot believe that all my friends too! My manager, Alesia, comes every other week or so with proceeds from the fundraisers my job has held for me in my honor. Also, two of my high school friends, Sherry and Carolyn, has come to visit me. One of them comes all the way from Maryland, and the other comes from Texas. These two ladies I have not seen in many years! I am talking about way back in the day! I sit there, thinking, *God, I am so blessed. Even they thought to come visit me!*

Every day, I wake up and use my walker to go to the bathroom downstairs to brush my teeth, wash up, change my pajamas, try to eat something, watch the same programs on TV, and fall asleep. That is my daily routine. Boooring! So the next day, I say to myself, *I have got to get up from here and do something*, but my daughter Kisha, who has now moved in with me, has kept close watch over me. Also, not to mention, the rest of my family does too, and they come daily! Because of that, it seems impossible for me to get up and do anything without them noticing. Plus, the medication is keeping me sleepy, so I cannot really get up and do much of anything, but I feel like I could.

The next day, my mother comes over to take me to the neurosurgeon so that I can have my halo adjusted and tightened and to also have my staples removed. I have sixty-two stitches removed from my neck and back. It is not painful having them removed, but that sure is a lot of stitches! Once the nurse has removed the stitches, I ask if my mom can clean my back, and she replies, "Yes, that will be fine," but she can only use a damp towel to wipe me with before they have to put the halo back on. It feels so good when my mother wipes my back; it has been a long time since my back has been washed.

The following day in the afternoon, my mom is back to do her daily visit with me, and she must have felt a little sorry for me because she asks me if I want to get out of the house and go get something to eat for lunch. I answer "Yes, I would like that." So here I go with my walker to her car; I am trying to get into the car, but this doggone halo is not really fitting in! We put the back of the passenger seat all the way down, and now I can fit inside, and my seat belt is fastened. I am happy to be outside and out of the house once again, so I am ready to go! A little uncomfortable but happy! We go and grab some fish and chips, which is so delicious!

We go back to my house, and when I get out of the car, I tell my mother that I no longer want to walk with the walker. She tells me, "Yes, you have to walk with it, or else you will fall." I tell her that I know I can walk without it. So I show her on the way walking to my house (several feet away) that I can walk without it, and then I tell her that I am no longer going to use it anymore nor become dependent to it. I promise that I will take my time and walk without it, and that is just what I did.

From that moment on, I walk around the house without it. Now when I walk to the bathroom, I look up at the stairs, and I say to myself, *One day, I am going to walk up these stairs and go to my bedroom.*

Chapter 7

———— ✑ ————

These days, I am starting to feel a lot stronger, and I am slowly getting my appetite back. I have still been walking without the walker—I take daily walks back and forth to the mailbox for my exercise for the day. I realize the reason I am sleeping so much is due to all the medication that I must take. I decide that I am going to take myself off some of the medication a little at a time. Every time my mother or my daughter gives me my daily dosages, I only bite half of the pills and throw the other half in the trash just to see how I will feel, or how much pain I can tolerate. Once I know I can do well with only half of the pills, I then begin to take one-fourth of the pills. If the pain gets too much for me, then I will take a higher dosage, of course. I have found out I am able to stay awake a lot longer with very minimal pain.

When I wake up in the morning, my new routine is first, thank God for waking me up, and then I brush my teeth, wash up, eat, watch TV, and then walk to the mailbox for my exercise. This time, when I go to the mailbox, I have a bunch of cards and letters from my coworkers and friends. I am so excited that I cannot wait to walk back home and read all of this. I get cards, letters, and gift cards! I read each one of them, one at a time. There is one card that stands out to me. Although I appreciate all of them, this one card has caught my eye more than the others. The name on this card I have recognized. So I ask my daughter for some paper and tell her where to find my envelopes and bring them to me, and she does. I sit on my hospital bed and answer every card and letter that I have received. The one that I mention that has a name on it that I recognize or have heard about, I save for last. My sister told me that she received a call from my station manager from work who indicated that a man who was a mechanic for Southwest Airlines was at the accident. She said she could not remember the name of the person at that time, but she had mentioned his name to me earlier on to let me know that he was trying to reach out to me. So when I receive this card from a Mike Mcgovern, I know I have not work with this person, so it has to be the guy that is possibly at the accident. I send him a thank-you card, as I did to all the others, and then I write him a note, asking him to give me a call.

One day I am sitting up in my hospital bed watching television when my phone rings. It is Mike. He asks how I am doing. "I am doing good," I reply. He sighs, and it almost sounds like he may have been crying. I say to him, "I have a question to ask you."

And he says, "Okay, what is it?"

I say, "Were you at the accident, and are you the man who had my granddaughter in your arms, and do you have a bunch of curly white hair?"

He chuckles and says, "Well, I have some gray hair, and yes, I am the one who took your granddaughter from the car."

I gasp. I ask him if she was holding him for dear life. He says yes, and in fact, she did not want him to put her down. So I thank him very much for what he has done. He begins to cry, so I ask what is wrong. He says he is glad to hear my voice and to know that I am doing well. I begin to cry also because I know he is thinking that I did not make it out from the accident. There is something about his spirit that touches me. He is so soft-spoken and gentle-sounding; I know I have to meet him. I tell him that when I get the halo taken off my head and body, I will come to visit him so that we can meet in person. He agrees.

As I am sitting in my hospital bed, I start thinking about Mike, and I wonder what has happened to all the others who helped us at the accident. Did anyone get their names? I ask Tommy; he does not know, so I ask my daughters if they have any idea who the others are, or if they have gathered any phone numbers, anything. None of them has any idea whom the people I call my angels are. When

I get up the next morning, I thought to contact the news, in hopes that they will be able to help me possibly locate these people, but the only name I can remember is Michelle. So I do not have much to go on. I tell the person who works for the news station and the one who answered my email regarding the accident all that I know and asks him if he can help me in finding these people. They play such an important role in my surviving, and I want to personally thank each one of them for all that they did to help me and my family at the accident. He lets me know that this is a very touching story, and that he will get back with me, which he never does.

My three months are up, and today is the day that I go get my halo off. I cannot wait for it to go! But wait…without this halo, am I going to be able to hold my head up? Will I be stiff? Am I going to be able to dance? What is it going to be like without it? All these thoughts are running through my mind. My father and stepmother arrive at my house to take me to the neurosurgeon to be checked and have the halo removed. When the doctor comes into the office, he checks me over, and then he begins to remove my halo. I ask him if I am going to be a bobblehead. He says, "No, you will be more like a stiff head!"

It feels very weird trying to walk without it. In fact, I do not know how to hold my head up while walking; it seems as though I am walking crooked and off-balance. So my stepmother and I are laughing because I am looking around at other people to see how they are holding their heads, making sure that I am holding mine correctly. I say, "This is going to take practice for me to get this head right!"

At night, when I would lay down to go to sleep, I find it exceedingly difficult to do so. It feels a lot better sleeping with the halo. It is so painful! I try every pillow that I could try to make it more comfortable for me to sleep. It is not working, and I am not sleeping. Also, trying to adjust to my new lifestyle is not easy.

When I wake up the next morning, I decide to call to have the hospital bed picked up and have my living room furniture put back together the way it used to be. I am not receiving visitors as much as I did in the past because I am doing a lot better and pretty much self-sufficient. I am always trying to talk my daughter into going back to her own house and living her life as she should before my accident took place. My daughter does leave to go check on her house and run some errands. While she is away and there is no one else around, I decide that I am going to go upstairs to my bedroom. I take one step at a time, going as slow as I possibly could not to hurt myself or fall. I made it! I am upstairs and in my room! It is so nice to be up here! I turn on my TV, and then I lay on my California king-size bed. I get in the shower and stay in there until all the hot water is running out! It feels so good to be in my room. Now I am thinking, *Yeah, it feels good to be upstairs in my bedroom, but I will eventually need to go back down the stairs because I will need something to eat and drink*. I take my time holding on to the rails, and I walk back down the stairs. Still immensely proud of myself that I am now able to walk up and down the stairs slowly, and I can start sleeping on my own bed.

Chapter 8

— ❧ —

I am getting outside of the house a little more these days since I am
not wearing the halo any longer. I am also able to drive myself
around, and I am still watching other people how they hold their
heads so that I can practice holding my head the same way. That way,
I can feel like I am looking normal. It is still a little difficult for me,
but I just keep practicing.

I want to make a trip to the airport to take cake and cookies to
my coworkers and thank them for everything that they did for me
during my hardship at home. I am also very anxious to meet with
Mike. So when I arrive at the airport, I am greeted by a lot of my fel-
low coworkers, and it is so good to see them all! A lot of them cannot
believe that I am up walking around and have made it there to see
them. I am asked by so many of them as to when I will be return-
ing to work. I tell them that by the end of the year, I would return
because I am feeling a lot better.

Now it is time to go meet Mike. I have made a call to him to tell
him where to meet me, and he does. I tell him what I am wearing so
that it will be easier for him to find me. When he walks up to me, I
look at him. I am incredibly happy to meet him and see him for that
matter, but I am confused! This is not the man that I saw holding my
granddaughter. So we hug each other for a long time; we even shed
a few tears together. He keeps looking at me in disbelief, and I am
looking at him the same way. He is looking at me because he cannot
believe that I am alive, and I am looking at him confused because
clearly, he is not the man whom I saw.

We talk for a while, and I have pictures of the accident that I show to him. He points himself out on the picture and says, "There I am with the hat on." I am thinking to myself, *How can that be?* Surely, he knows that he got my granddaughter out of the car, and I do not believe that he will tell a lie about that. It is noticeably clear that he was there at the scene of the accident because I can see him on the pictures. But again, that is not the man I saw holding my granddaughter. This man barely has hair! The most confusing part about this is that he had on a hat! The man I saw, did not have a hat on; he had a lot of curly white hair, and he was big! I am trying to explain to him what I saw, and he is looking at me with a confused look. He shrugs his shoulders to insinuate, *Well this is me, and I am the one that had your granddaughter.* He also helped Tommy and did whatever else he could do to be of help. *How do you explain that?* I think to myself. I am almost afraid to mention this to people because they will probably think that I have lost my ever-loving mind! I know what I saw, and he is not it! We say our goodbyes and promise to stay in contact with each other. I have a headache, and I am getting tired. I need to get back home to take a pain pill and get some rest.

I wake up today and have an appointment with the neurosurgeon's disability doctor. He is to analyze me and determine whether I will be able to return to work. I go inside and meet with this doctor, and I do all his exercises that he asks me to. Some of them I can complete, while some I cannot. He then sits down on his chair at his desk, and he begins to type on his desktop computer. He starts asking me questions regarding my job duties as to what I do daily. Again, he starts typing on his computer, so I am watching and waiting for his next reaction. He then turns to me and tells me that I will never be able to work again. I am dumbfounded! I just know I am feeling better, doing better, and can return to work. I say to him, "What do you mean I can't work?" *I just told everyone I would be back by the end of the year!* This is what I thought to myself. But this man has just told me that I will never be able to do that type of work again! "I love my job!" I yelled, "and I love the people whom I work with, and you are saying that I can no longer do that again!"

He replied, "No, you cannot."

I burst into tears and start sobbing! He apologizes to me for having to inform me of the news, which was awfully bad news to me. I leave his office devastated! I cry all the way home. When I get home, I go straight upstairs to my room. I have to ponder and digest all of this that I have just heard, and because of the accident, I will not be able to work in my current job again. I begin to look at my situation and the state I am in, wondering what I am supposed to do financially or just with my life, period! Then I think about my situation again. This time, instead of feeling sorry for myself or being disappointed with the fact that I cannot work, I begin to cry because I recognize how truly blessed I am that my God has spared, not only me, but Tommy and all three of my grandchildren as well. There is a reason why we survived that accident—I have a divine purpose in this earth. He is not through with me yet. I mean, I think about everything that I can possibly remember about the accident.

I start thinking about when we stopped to fill our tank up with gas. Why didn't the truck blow up, explode, or catch on fire when the tire blew out, and why we went over a guard rail down a mountain? It was certainly full of gas, especially after flipping so many times. And you think he doesn't exist? Why was my grandson ejected from the car and landed on a nearby rock? It is because if he had not been ejected, the side of the truck where he had been seated that caved in could have killed him! And you think he doesn't exist? Oh yeah, I remember Jamari was pinned inside of the truck, his lip was slashed, and he had cuts and bruises, but he was kept stable, unmovable until help arrived. And you think he doesn't exist? Then I watched Tommy in so much pain, not knowing his back was broken but having enough strength to climb out of the window to find my grandson, broken back and all! And you think he doesn't exist? Jaiouni, my granddaughter, did not have anything wrong with her at all. Surely, you will think that she would have had some type of injury, and at four years old I mentioned she said Grandma had her. Well I guess Grandma did have her because she was simply fine. And you think he doesn't exist? Then what about all the angels who were driving behind us—the doctor, the nurse, the fireman, and the two EMTs? Who would be so blessed to have all those people driving behind you, stopping and offering their help to take care of us until help arrived? That was a blessing within itself! And you think he doesn't exist?

Now here I am. Yes, I broke my neck, back, and ribs, and I may be put together by titanium rods and a bunch of other nuts, bolts, and screws, but I am alive, walking and talking! I may not be able to reach up with my arms like I used to, but I have use of both my arms and hands. I start thinking about all the things that I used to do, and I cannot do any longer—they all seem so minute now. I realize that you should never take anything for granted because it can be here today and gone tomorrow. How can I not feel so grateful and blessed after realizing all that he has done for me? All I could think of is a certain part of the serenity prayer, "God, grant me the serenity to accept the things I cannot change, courage to change the things I can." *It is okay*, I say to myself. *I am where I am meant to be.*

Chapter 9

───────── ❧ ─────────

Although I have accepted the fact that I am where I am meant to be, something in the back of my mind still wants to prove that I will be able to work again. So I keep working on my hand and arms, trying to gain strength, thinking to myself that I will not be defeated. I continue walking so that my legs will get stronger. I have pretty much quit taking a lot of the medication that I am on; I switch to nonnarcotic pain medicine because I do not want to get addicted to any of the narcotics that was prescribed to me. I only take medicine when I am feeling too much pain that I cannot handle. For the most part, I try to tough through the pain.

I make another appointment with the disability doctor to have him analyze me again. He has me do the same exercises, and this time, I am a lot stronger. He cannot believe it! He checks his paperwork to compare how I did the last time I was in his office, which is approximately a year or longer. He asks again what type of work I am doing; I explain to him again my job duties. Then he asks if there is anything that I can do, like some type of light duty. I tell him no because I have already inquired about that previously. Besides, I do not want to do light duty; I want to do the same job I have been doing, the job I have enjoyed doing!

So I asked him if he thinks that I am strong enough to return to my current position. He checks all his paperwork and starts typing on his computer of course. And then he starts recording himself talking on his little tape recorder about my health and the progress I have made, and he says, "Yes, I do believe you are able to go back to work now."

I scream, "Yes!" Then I jump up and hug him and say, "Thank you." I asks him how long I have to wait before I can return, and he says immediately, that he does not know any reason that will stop me from starting now.

This time, I leave that office skipping and jumping, thanking God the whole way to my car. As soon as I get inside of my car, I immediately call my manager and let him know that I am able to come back to work. He is so excited! He asks that I fax over the doctor's note stating that I am released to return to work. Then he connects me to the administrative department so they can give me a schedule, and I will be able to start working within the next three days. That is the best news I have heard in a long time. I also call my mother and tell her the good news! She cannot believe it, and she is so happy for me. She says to me, "God is so good!"

And I reply, "Yes, he is."

I return to work as planned, and of course, I have to go through some additional training due to having been out so long, but that is fine. I am anxious to get started and see if I will be able to still perform all my job duties. I am able to do it all! Some days are good, and some days are challenging, but I made it!

If you are ever traveling via Southwest Airlines and you are in the city of Phoenix, come and check me out, because that is where I will be—right back at work. And you think he doesn't exist? Praise God, amen!

Notes

I want to let you know that I feel inspired to write this book while sitting in my hospital bed. I have initially handwritten the book on paper because I did not own a computer at that time, where I could type everything. I have paper notes all over in hopes of putting them altogether one day so that I will be able to share my true thoughts of what I have experienced in a book.

Let me acknowledge these scriptures: Psalms 62:1 (NIV) and Revelations 1:12–14.

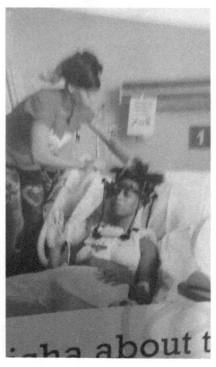

AND YOU THINK HE DOESN'T EXIST

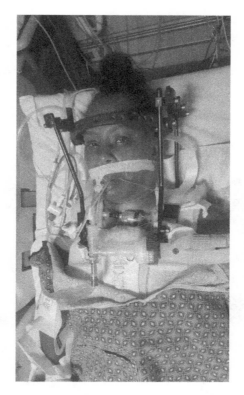

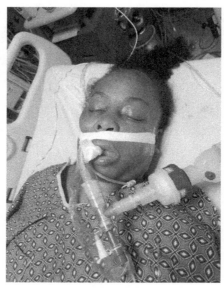

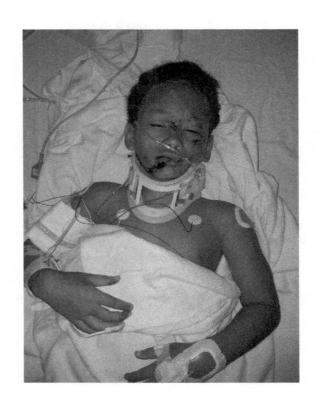

About the Author

Michelle Love is a first-time writer and author of And You Think He Doesn't Exist. She was born and raised in Albuquerque, New Mexico, and then later, her parents moved her to Phoenix, Arizona, on her senior year in high school (Imagine that!). Besides graduating from the school of cosmetology and working for one of the best companies in the world, she has hopes of becoming one of the best-selling authors.

In her spare time, Michelle enjoys karaoke, dancing, and spending time with her three adult children, nine grandchildren, and her wonderful husband. She is a lover of pot-bellied pigs!